CW00554952

the worm turneth ↄↄ
the patient will be whole
again

MEMORIOUS EARTH

A LONGITUDINAL STUDY

A. Richardson & R. Skelton

XYLEM BOOKS 2018

Memorious Earth, A Longitudinal Study

Copyright © Autumn Richardson
& Richard Skelton 2010–2017
The authors' moral rights have been asserted

First published in 2015 by Corbel Stone Press
This edition copyright © Xylem Books 2018

ISBN: 978-1-9999718-4-7

Xylem Books is an imprint of Corbel Stone Press

INTRODUCTION

Devoke Water, Cumbria, UK. A tarn hidden from the view of a lonely, high road that connects two valleys in the backcountry between the Irish Sea and the peaks of Great Gable and Scafell. A region of crags and scars, heather and bracken, grassland and bogs. The name *Devoke* is itself unusual and strangely compelling – perhaps because it contains the word *evoke*: to conjure, summon, bring forth. Befitting its veiled position, its etymology is obscure – some have thought it refers to a personal name of Norse origin, *Duffock's Water*. Others ascribe it to the oldest strata of Celtic languages in Britain, reconstructing it as **dubāco* or **dubācā, the dark one*. In the written record the name has undergone centuries of transformation – *Duuok, Duffok, Dudock, Denok, Dovic, Devock, Duvvock* – a textual echo of broader changes visited upon the land itself.

Among the hills that cluster around the tarn is *Ulpha Fell*, a name which also applies to a village in the nearby Duddon valley. Like Devoke, it too has ambiguous origins. Again, there is a Norse connection, *Ulfr haugr – Ulf's hill or burial mound*. In 1777, Nicolson & Burn[1] wrote: 'Upon the north side of Millum [*sic*], up the river of Duddon, lies Ulpha or Ouffa, among the rocky hills, which was granted, as is before mentioned, to Ulfe, who gave name to the place.' However, modern scholars, including Bruce Dickins and Diana Whaley,[2] have noted a connection with the animal from which Ulf(e) took his name, the wolf itself. *Ulfr haugr – hill of the wolf*. There are other toponyms in the area that might affirm this connection – to the south-east is *Ulgra Beck, stream by the wolf-pits*,[3] and to the east is *Dog How, hill of the dog* (the epithet *dog* often being given to the male wolf).

Along with lynx and bear, the wolf has long been extinct in England – actual dates vary from county to county, but in Cumbria it is thought to have been extirpated by the 15th century.[4] The land-names surrounding Devoke Water bear testimony to many more species of animal and plant that no longer exist there, or endure in pitifully small numbers. They are little more than ghosts; reminders of a vanished epoch. Among them are *deer* (Harter Fell), *lapwing* (Tewit Moss), *pine marten* (Mart Crag), *red kite* (Kitt How), *snake* (Wormshell How), *alder* (Ellerbeck Bridge), *birch* (Birker Fell), *lime* (Linbeck Gill), *holly* (Hollin How) and *rowan* (Rowantree How).

This place-name evidence is corroborated in no small measure by modern archaeological and palynological surveys, which seek to decode the testimonies of the land itself. The *Duddon Valley Local History Group*, among others, have reported a broad narrative of ecological succession for the area, beginning around 12,000 years ago[5] with its slow emergence from beneath the receding ice sheets – a post-glacial desert that was gradually recolonised by grasses, docks, herbaceous plants and dwarf shrubs. Eventually this tundra-like environment gave way to birch and willow, reaching an apex of mixed deciduous woodland by around 7,000 years ago, with trees covering the entire upland landscape surrounding Devoke Water, and extending to 750 metres above sea-level in even higher ground, covering all but the tallest peaks in the Lake District region.

When faced with the exposed, weathered contours of the present day Birker and Ulpha Fell, it is difficult to imagine them once covered with swathes of oak, birch, hazel and beech. In 1777, Nicolson & Burn wrote 'the lower part of Ulpha is very woody and good land, the upper part more rocky and barren.' It is this environmental degradation – with the loss of so many plant and animal species – which stimulated our initial study of the area, commencing with came to the attention of Nick Rogers at *Lakeland Arts*, the charity which manages several historic buildings in Cumbria, including *Abbot Hall Art Gallery* and *Blackwell, the Arts and Crafts House*. Nick generously invited us to exhibit at both spaces, and in early 2015 we presented *Memorious Earth: A Longitudinal Study* – a retrospective exhibition incorporating music, film, printed matter, objects and artefacts.

Some of the objects we exhibited included many glass phials and bottles of natural particulae: wind-blown seeds, leaf fragments, grass stalks, small stones, bark and feathers found on our many explorations of the uplands. For us these artefacts are a vital testimony of the land itself; they are voices in an infinite polyphony – *a singing of minutiae*.

Our use of glass vessels is partly an aesthetic device to draw attention to the beauty and fragility of these natural artefacts – the glass itself acting as a kind of lens, giving greater focus; asking for attention. Moreover, in 'over protecting' such seemingly inconsequential and naturally bountiful objects, we are asking for a re-evaluation of their worth, especially considering that they may not always be so plentiful. This is particularly true in cases such as the *English bluebell*, which is in widespread decline. When presented in the context of poems such as *Relics*, the picture we are trying to create is one of a continual environmental flux in which humankind plays a determining role.

It is also worth mentioning that our use of phials and bottles isn't merely aesthetic – their apothecarial quality alludes to the medicinal properties of the plants themselves, and our use of seeds references the movement within environmentalism called 'seed saving' – building a living archive of indigenous plants as a way of trying to maintain biodiversity and mitigate the effects of GMOs, plant patenting, etc.

Nevertheless, making work with, and exhibiting, these natural objects is not unproblematic. There is, for example, an unwelcome connection to the history of scientific specimen hunting which reached its apotheosis in the Victorian age. Our efforts could therefore be misinterpreted, especially as our word-lists could be seen to be celebrating the taxonomising of the natural world – an endeavour which, for us, reduces life to a series of hierarchical relations. Although we do use scientific source material, our repurposing of it is intended to draw attention to the seemingly small, the overlooked or misunderstood.

Both our written and assemblage work is therefore involved in a critical dialogue with its own contexts and historical precedents – the act of naming is a form of recognition, but taxonomy can also obfuscate, drawing attention away from *things* to *concepts*. Moreover, words themselves can be a means of control – the facility of language to *define* can lead to a form of possession, of *capture*, but all definitions inherently limit subtlety and complexity, diminishing uniqueness through the equation with an archetype. As Laurie Clark so beautifully demonstrates in her buttercups and harebells series of drawings,[7] each plant of the same species, whilst bearing common traits, is itself exquisitely singular. What botanists such as Bentham and Hooker[8] call 'aberrations' (i.e. instances of deviation from the botanical norm) are perhaps an outward signifier of Gerard Manley Hopkins' term *inscape* – the individual identity, the *isness*, of each living thing.

*

We would like to thank everyone who has supported our work in Cumbria for the past five years. Especial thanks go to Robert Macfarlane (not least for inadvertently providing the title *Memorious Earth*), to Mark Valentine for his fascinating research into wolf folklore, to Nick Rogers and everyone at *Lakeland Arts*, to Carol Davies at *Kendal Museum* for the generous loan of a wolf skeleton, to Craig Taylor and Simon Prosser at *Five Dials* magazine, to Andrew Forster and Jeff Cowton at *The Wordsworth Trust*, to Sharon Blackie at *Earthlines* magazine, and to Mike Collier at *W.A.L.K.*

Autumn Richardson & Richard Skelton
Cumbria, June, 2015

NOTES

1. *The History and Antiquities of the Counties of Cumberland and Westmorland*, Volume II, Joseph Nicolson & Richard Burn, 1777.
2. *The Place-Names of Cumberland*, Bruce Dickins, Ed., 1950; A Dictionary of Lake District Place-Names, Diana Whaley, 2006.
3. This place-name is mentioned by neither Dickins nor Whaley. The first element, *Ulgra*, is possibly a corruption of the ON *ulfr* 'wolf' and *grof* 'pit'.
4. *The Last Wolf in England, In Folklore and Fiction*, Mark Valentine, *Reliquiae*, Volume Two, 2014. Local folklore also tells of a wolf in connection with the place-name *Lady's Dub*, a deep pool in the river Duddon below Rainsbarrow Wood in which a gentlewoman is reputed to have lost her life, supposedly whilst being pursued by the animal.
5. *Ring Cairns to Reservoirs: Archaeological Discoveries in the Dudden Valley, Cumbria*, Duddon Valley Local History Group, 2009. See also *Tarns of the Central Lake District*, Haworth et al, 2003. The DVLHG do not cite their source for the estimate of 12,000 years, but it is most likely measured in radiocarbon years. Due to fluctuations in the levels of ^{14}C isotopes over millennia, the actual date may therefore be much earlier.
6. See the notes to *Relics* in this book for a discussion of the absolute 'local' presence of plant genera indicated by pollen.
7. *100 Buttercups*, Laurie Clark, 2011 and *100 Harebells*, Laurie Clark, 2012.
8. *Handbook of the British Flora*, George Bentham & J.D. Hooker, 1937.

5.

Grasses, sedge and bracken
recover the rootless
felled expanses.

They break ground
for birch, for oak –

finding tenure in a
skin of soil.

6.

Stone packed into stone. Rough
cradle for heather, for bracken.

Black crags insinuated with
stone-crop and rock-rose.

A region for crows, for storm,
tenanted by *meadow* and *quaking* and *blue;*

A waste of blades forged in
sunlight and wind.

7.

A LIST OF PROBABLE GRASSES

Common Bent Grass *Agrostis tenuis,*
Silvery Hair-grass *Aira caryophyllea,*
Early Hair-grass *Aira praecox,*
Sweet Vernal-grass *Anthoxanthum
odoratum,* Fern Grass *Catapodium
rigidum,* Blue Moor-grass *Sesleria
caerulea,* Common Quaking-grass
Briza media, Wavy Hair-grass
Deschampsia flexuosa, Fine-leaved
Sheep's Fescue *Festuca tenuifolia,*
Brome Fescue *Vulpia bromoides,*
Sheep's Fescue *Festuca ovina,* Strong
Creeping Red Fescue *Festuca rubra
rubra,* Annual Meadow-grass *Poa
annua,* Tufted or Meadow Soft-
grass *Holcus lanatus,* Purple Moor-
grass *Molinia caerulea,* Mat-grass
Nardus stricta, Smooth Meadow-
grass *Poa pratensis.*

8.

Duvokeswater c. [1205]

Duuokwat [1279]

Duffokiswatir c. [1280]

Devoke [1626]

Dovic Water [1769]

Devocke Water [1860]

9.

NEAR WATNESS COY

Alone –
the woven isle.

A clutch for roots and spires within
ever-changing waters.
A last arboreal hold before barren slopes.

The last stand of all that's fallen.

10.

Set like seeds into the fell
above the little dark are stones –

gray weights within a sea of
whins and reeds.

*

Beneath rest those of
an earth once birched,

and their forests, fallen,
feed the roots of grasses.

11.

Raised above *Devoke Water*.
Along *Water Crag, Pike How*
    and *Hall Beck*.

Scattered above *High Ground*.
along *Ladder Crag, Rough Crag*
    and *White Wall*.

Left below *The Seat*.
along *Sike Moss, Brown Rigg*
    and *Crosby Gill*.

12.

GIFT

Where
the rowan grows through
touch, fissures become

　　　becks rivulets gills

shimmed with light, as snow
gives way to sun.

13.

Gorse is the Ever-flower
        wedded to waste places.

Heather is the Brush-flower
        dry sea of violet.

Yew is the Stone-clasp
        reconciled to stone.

Bracken is the Red-wrack
        cast upon the fells.

14.

Haugr, the grave mound, hill or heel
dim shape of rest.

Sker, the isolated rock, peak or cliff
broken face of grey.

Fjall, the mountain, height or moor
high tumbling meadow.

Bekkr, the stream or little river
small rain in the narrow ravine.

15.

No voice but in the tongues
of others
no weight but in the pull
of mountains

> *placeless*
> *breath-stealer*
> *never dwelling*

a form less
clothed than air
tirelessly stitching-unstitching
hill side, moor and fell.

16.

Host to revenant skins –
departed stands of birch

and oak and holly – their bones
became the birthing saps for grasses.

Now this terrestrial sea.
These stalks wave-shaped by winds

decay and ready the earth
for birch again.

17.

Harter Fell, a memory;
    the hill bereft of deer.

Birker Fell, an echo;
    the hill absented by birch.

Ulpha Fell, a reproach;
    the hill silenced of wolves.

18.

THE BRIGHT ONE

The beginning; the inception;
the medicine stirrings of earth.

*

The rowan seed, cased
in cold soils, stirs; a tiny
fist unfurls – muscles
upwards – piercing crust.
A translucent filament seeks
the sun. Sips from melting drifts.

WOLF NOTES

by Autumn Richardson & Richard Skelton, 2010

BIBLIOGRAPHY

- Bonnier, Gaston, 1925, *British Flora*
- Cherry, J., 1961, *Cairns of the Birker Fell and Ulpha Fell Area*
- Dickins, Bruce, (Ed.), 1950, *The Place-Names of Cumberland*
- Dickinson, William, 1878, *A Glossary of Words and Phrases Pertaining to the Dialect of Cumberland*
- Duddon Valley Local History Group, 2009, *Ring Cairns to Reservoirs: Archaeological Discoveries in the Duddon Valley, Cumbria*
- Ekwall, Eilert, 1922, *The Place-Names of Lancashire*
- Prevost, E.W., 1905, *A Supplement to the Glossary of the Dialect of Cumberland*
- Whaley, Diana, 2006, *A Dictionary of Lake District Place-Names*

A LIST OF PROBABLE FLORA

2 0 1 3

Alder	Blackthorn
Wood anemone	Brittle bladder-fern*
Wild angelica	Blinks
Marsh arrow-grass	Bluebell
Ash	Bogbean
Bog asphodel	Bracken
*Water avens	Bramble*
*Wood avens	Soft brome
Heath bedstraw	Brooklime*
Marsh bedstraw	Broad buckler-fern
*Beech	Narrow buckler-fern*
Besser	Bugle
Betony	Lesser burdock*
Bilberry	Great burnet*
Downy birch	Bulbous buttercup*
Silver birch	Creeping buttercup
Hairy bitter-cress	Meadow buttercup
Wavy bitter-cress	Common butterwort

*Red campion	Lesser clubmoss
Cat's ear	Stag's-horn clubmoss*
Cat's-tail	Cock's-foot
Smaller cat's-tail	Common cotton-grass
Lesser celandine	Hare's-tail cotton-grass
*Wild chamomile	Cowberry*
*Charlock	Cranberry
Wild cherry	Wood cranesbill*
Rough chervil	Thale cress*
*Horse chestnut	Water cress*
*Sweet chestnut	Crowberry
Common chickweed	Ivy-leaved crowfoot*
Common mouse-ear chickweed	Marsh cudweed
Sticky mouse-ear chickweed	Red currant
*Marsh cinquefoil	Daisy
Red clover	Ox-eye daisy
White clover	Dandelion
Fir clubmoss	Broad-leaved dock

*Curled dock	Viviparous sheep's fescue*
Common dog-violet	Cuckoo flower
Crested dog's-tail	Creeping forget-me-not
Elder	Field forget-me-not
Eyebright	Tufted forget-me-not
Beech fern	Water forget-me-not
Hard fern	Foxglove
Hart's-tongue fern	Marsh foxtail
Lady fern	Wild garlic*
Lemon-scented mountain fern	Globeflower*
Male fern	Goldenrod
Oak fern	Gooseberry
Parsley fern	Whin gorse
Wilson's filmy fern	Western gorse
*Giant fescue	Grass of parnassus*
Meadow fescue	Annual meadow-grass
Red fescue	Brown bent grass
Sheep's fescue	Common bent grass

Creeping bent grass	Marsh hawk's-beard*
Creeping soft-grass	Autumnal hawkbit
Deer grass	Rough hawkbit*
Early hair-grass	Hawthorn
False oat-grass	Hazel
Heath grass	Cross-leaved heath
Mat grass	Ling heather
Quaking grass	Bell heather
Rough meadow-grass	Fat hen
Silver hair-grass	Hogweed
Smooth meadow-grass	Holly
Sweet vernal grass	Honeysuckle
Tufted hair-grass	Field horsetail
Velvet grass	Water horsetail
Wavy hair-grass	Ivy
*Wood groundsel	Jack-by-the-hedge*
*Groundsel	Juniper
Harebell	Lesser knapweed

Knotweed	Nipplewort*
European larch	Pedunculate oak
Water lobelia	Sessile oak
Lousewort	Common orache*
*Marsh lousewort	Heath spotted-orchid
Scaly male-fern	Upright hedge-parsley*
Marsh marigold	Procumbent pearlwort
Rayless mayweed	Marsh pennywort
*Lesser meadow-rue	Water pepper
Meadowsweet	Pale persicaria
*Wood melick	Pignut*
Heath milkwort	Bog pimpernel
Water mint	Scarlet pimpernel*
Purple moor-grass	Yellow pimpernel
*Hedge mustard	Scots pine
Bog myrtle	Greater plantain
*Navelwort	Ribwort plantain
Common hemp-nettle	Polypody
Stinging nettle	Bog pondweed

Broad-leaved pondweed	Guelder rose*
*Red pondweed	Roseroot*
Welsh poppy	Rowan
Primrose	Wall rue
Shepherd's purse	Bristle club-rush
*Pink purslane	Bulbous rush
Quillwort	Common spike-rush
Ragwort	Field wood-rush
Marsh ragwort	Floating club-rush*
Oxford ragwort	Great wood-rush
Raspberry	Heath rush
Yellow rattle	Heath wood-rush
Redshank	Jointed rush
Common reed	Many-stalked spike-rush
Floating bur-reed	Soft rush
Rhododendron	Toad rush
Herb robert	Perennial rye-grass
Ragged robin	Wood sage
Dog rose	Three-nerved sandwort*

Opposite-leaved golden-saxifrage	Tawny sedge
Starry saxifrage	White beak-sedge
Yellow mountain saxifrage	White sedge*
Devil's-bit scabious	Wood sedge*
Bottle sedge	Hard shield-fern*
Carnation sedge	Shore-weed
Common sedge	Silverweed*
Dioecious sedge	Sneezewort
Few-flowered sedge	Common sorrel
Flea sedge	Sheep's sorrel
*Glaucous sedge	Wood-sorrel
Green-ribbed sedge	Lesser spearwort
Oval sedge	Buxbaum's speedwell*
*Pale sedge	Common speedwell*
Pill sedge	Grey speedwell*
*Remote sedge	Thyme-leaved speedwell
*Smooth sedge	Wall speedwell
Spring sedge	Maidenhair spleenwort
Star sedge	Corn spurrey

Slender St. John's wort	Greater bird's-foot trefoil
*Trailing St. John's wort	Lesser trefoil*
Common water-starwort	Valerian
Bog stitchwort	Marsh valerian*
Greater stitchwort	Tufted vetch*
Lesser stitchwort	Marsh violet
*Biting stonecrop	Fool's water-cress*
English stonecrop	Alternate water-milfoil*
*Rock stonecrop	American willow-herb*
*Barren strawberry	Broad-leaved willow-herb*
*Wild strawberry	Great hairy willow-herb*
Sundew	Marsh willow-herb
Sycamore	Rosebay willow-herb
Creeping thistle	Creeping willow
Marsh thistle	Eared willow
Spear thistle	Goat willow*
Wild thyme	Grey willow
Tormentil	Marsh woundwort*
Common bird's-foot trefoil	Yarrow

A LIST OF PROBABLE FLORA

by Autumn Richardson & Richard Skelton, 2013

NOTE

Asterisks (*) indicate rare species.

BIBLIOGRAPHY

°   Halliday, Geoffrey, 1997, *A Flora of Cumbria*

.

RELICS

2013

ALDER
Alnus

1. Proto-Indo-European 2. Proto-Germanic 3. Old English 4. Old Norse
5. Middle English 6. English Dialect 7. Modern English

ASH

Fraxinus

1. Proto-Indo-European 2. Proto-Germanic 3. Old English 4. Old Norse
5. Middle English 6. English Dialect 7. Modern English

BEECH

Fagus

1. Proto-Indo-European 2. Proto-Germanic 3. Old English 4. Old Norse
5. Middle English 6. English Dialect 7. Modern English

BIRCH

Betula

1. Proto-Indo-European 2. Proto-Germanic 3. Old English 4. Old Norse
5. Middle English 6. English Dialect 7. Modern English

ELM

Ulmus

1. Proto-Indo-European 2. Proto-Germanic 3. Old English 4. Old Norse
5. Middle English 6. English Dialect 7. Modern English

HAZEL
Corylus

1. Proto-Indo-European 2. Proto-Germanic 3. Old English 4. Old Norse
5. Middle English 6. English Dialect 7. Modern English

JUNIPER

Juniperus

1. Proto-Indo-European 2. Proto-Germanic 3. Latin
4. Middle English 5. Modern English

LIME

Tilia

1. Proto-Indo-European 2. Proto-Germanic 3. Old English 4. Old Norse
5. Middle English 6. English Dialect 7. Modern English

OAK

Quercus

1. Proto-Germanic 2. Old English 3. Old Norse
4. Middle English 5. English Dialect 6. Modern English

PINE

Pinus

1. Proto-Indo-European 2. Latin 3. Old English
4. Middle English 5. Modern English

SALLOW
Salix

1. Proto-Indo-European 2. Proto-Germanic 3. Old English 4. Old Norse
5. Middle English 6. English Dialect 7. Modern English

WILLOW

Salix

1. Proto-Indo-European 2. Proto-Germanic 3. Old English 4. Old Norse
5 & 6. Middle English 7. English Dialect 8. Modern English

WYCH-ELM
Ulmus

1. Proto-Indo-European 2. Proto-Germanic 3. Old English
4. Middle English 5. English Dialect 6. Modern English

THE POLLEN RECORD FOR DEVOKE WATER [1]

Alnus	*Pinus*
Artemisia	Plantago
Betula	Plantago lanceolata
Calluna	Polypodium
Chenopodiaceæ	Potentilla
Chenopodium	Pteridium
Compositæ	*Quercus*
Coryloid [2]	Ranunculaceæ
Cruciferæ	Rosaceæ
Cyperaceæ	Rubiaceæ
Fagus	Rumex
Filicales	Rumex acetosella
Filipendula	*Salix*
Fraxinus	Scrophulariaceæ
Galium	Selaginella
Gramineæ	Sphagnum
Hedera	Succisa
Isoetes	Thalictrum
Juniperus	*Tilia*
Labiatæ	*Ulmus*
Lycopodium	Umbelliferæ

1. This list is a composite of two pollen diagrams published by Winifred Pennington (1964) from marginal and central core samples of Devoke Water. The classifications have been preserved here as published, although some may have since been subject to revision. The 'tree' genera are italicised.

2. According to Pennington, 'Coryloid' pollen, while predominantly that of *Corylus* (*Corylus avellana*; hazel), also includes some grains of *Myrica* (*Myrica gale*; bog myrtle).

NOTES

Salix appears as both *Willow* and *Sallow*; *Ulmus* as *Elm* and *Wych-Elm*.

The occurrence of pollen from tree genera in soil core samples does not necessarily indicate their absolute 'local' presence. Winifred Pennington, who published these findings, makes a special case for *Pinus*, whose occurrence may be the result of 'distant transport'. The term 'tree' itself is also problematic, as some genera, notably *Betula*, also contain shrub species such as *Betula nana*; dwarf birch.

The upland landscape around Devoke Water is not completely devoid of trees. The habitations of *Woodend* and *Birkerthwaite* (ON *birki* 'birch'; Gaelic-Norse *ærgi/erg* 'shieling'; ON *þveit* 'clearing') both have small wooded enclosures, although these are surely plantations rather than the remnants of prehistoric woodland.

The analogy between word-evolution and tree-growth is loose, as many closely related languages (such as Old English and Old Norse) developed concurrently, rather than sequentially. Old Norse has been included in these selections as it exerted a great influence on the toponymy and dialect of Cumbria. The English dialect is also referenced, but only those word-forms that are variations on the English common name for each tree.

Approximate dates for the various languages (excluding English dialect) are as follows:

Proto-Indo-European (pre-3rd millennium bc)
Proto-Germanic (500–100 BC)
Latin (c. 6th century BC–1800 AD)
Old English (600–1100 AD)
Old Norse (700–1300 AD)
Middle English (1100–1500 AD)
Modern English (1550 AD)

RELICS

by Autumn Richardson & Richard Skelton, 2013

BIBLIOGRAPHY

°   De Cleene, Marcel; Lejeune, Marie Claire, 2003, *Compendium of Symbolic and Ritual Plants in Europe*

°   Dickinson, William, 1878, *A Glossary of Words and Phrases Pertaining to the Dialect of Cumberland*

°   Fick, August; Falk, Hjalmar; Torp, Alf, 1909, *Wörterbuch der Indogermanischen Sprachen Dritter Teil: Wortschatz der Germanischen Spracheinheit*

°   McSparran, Frances, 2001, *The Middle English Compendium*

°   Nodal, John H.; Milner, George, 1875, *A Glossary of the Lancashire Dialect*

°   Pennington, Winifred, 1964, *Pollen Analyses from the Deposits of Six Upland Tarns in the Lake District*, Philosophical Transactions of the Royal Society of London. Series B, Biological sciences, Vol. 248, No. 746, pp. 205–244

°   Pennington, Winifred, 1970, *Vegetation History in the North-West of England : A Regional Synthesis*, Studies in the Vegetational History of the British Isles, Edited by D. Walker & R.G. West, pp. 41–79

°   Skeat, Walter W., 1882, *A Concise Etymological Dictionary of the English Language*

°   Vigfusson, Gudbrand, 1874, *An Icelandic-English Dictionary, based on the Manuscript Collections of the Late Richard Cleasby, Enlarged and Completed*

°   Watkins, Calvert, 2001, *The American Heritage Dictionary of Indo-European Roots*

WOLFHOU

2013

The Absented Bield and Other Songs

touch path
slope stirs
from memory
into carvings

1279

Duuokwat:
ice wolves. fells felled. filament rain.
seed memory. brythonic mosses.

Haugr:
cold cast
above meadow grass
rough grave
left to heather

1337

Birker:
where are the birch gatherings?
the fell oak expanses?

pale saps
seeds
rest in grasses
wolf barren

1449

Harter:
how is the deer rake left unattended?

dry
ravine
revenant path
to the sea

1695

Uffay:
the hill is echoless of wolves.
the brant earth silenced
of yew tongues.

1769

the fell wall stirs. muscles a rough way upwards.
tirelessly weights the waste. grows grey.
skins birch, rowan, heather.
seeks wolves.

1860

into the absented bield. the hill grave.
recover within fox memory. moss drifts.
brush soils last shaped by bracken.
worm ground. familial earth. ready.

WOLFHOU [10] [12]

1279

ULFHOU [8] [10] [12]

1337

ULPHO [10] [12]

1449

UFFAY [12]

1576

ULFHAY [7]

c. 1600

WOOLFHAY [12]

1610

UFFAY [1]

1610

ULPHA [10] [12]

1625

ULPHAY [10]

1638

ULFAY [4] [10]

1646

UFFAY [10]

1695

ULPHAY [3]

1770

OUFFA [4]

1777

ULFA [4]

1777

ULPHA [4]

1777

WOOLFHEY [4]

1777

ULPHA [5]

1823

DUVOKESWATER [9] [12]
c. 1205

DEVOKE [12]
1626

DUUOKWAT [12]
1279

DOVIC WATER [2]
1769

DUFFOKISWATIR [12]
c. 1280

DEVOCK LAKE [3]
1770

DUDOCKIS TERNE [11]
c. 13th century

DEVOCK WATER [5]
1823

FOSSE TERNE [11]
c. 13th century

DEVOCK WATER [6]
1860

DUÐOCKIS WATIR [9]
c. late 13th century

DEVOCKE WATER [6]
1860

DENOK FLU [1]
1610

DUVVOCK WATER [11]
c. 20th century

1. *John Speed's Map of Cumberland*, 1610.

2. *Manorial Title Deeds*, 1769.

3. *Thomas Donald's County of Cumberland Map*, 1770–1.

4. *The History and Antiquities of the Counties of Cumberland and Westmorland*, Volume II, Joseph Nicolson & Richard Burn, 1777.

5. *Greenwood's Map of Cumberland*, 1823.

6. *A Guide to the Mountains, Lakes and North-West Coast of England*, Mackenzie E. C. Walcott, 1860.

7. *An Accompt of the most considerable Estates and Families in the county of Cumberland*, John Denton of Cardew, Transactions of the Cumberland & Westmorland Antiquarian & Archaeological Society, 1887.

8. *The Place-Names of Cumberland and Westmorland*, W. J. Sedgefield, 1915.

9. *Some South Cumberland Place-Names*, Frank Warriner, Transactions of the Cumberland & Westmorland Antiquarian & Archaeological Society, NS XXVI, 1926.

10. *The Place-Names of Cumberland*, Bruce Dickins, Ed., 1950.

11. *The Tarns of Lakeland*, W. Heaton Cooper, 1960.

12. *A Dictionary of Lake District Place-Names*, Diana Whaley, 2006.

WOLFHOU

by Autumn Richardson & Richard Skelton, 2013

NOTE

Text assembled from the authors' previous work, *Wolf Notes*, 2010.

BIBLIOGRAPHY

- Denton, John, of Cardew, 1887, *An Accompt of the most considerable Estates and Families in the county of Cumberland*, Transactions of the Cumberland & Westmorland Antiquarian & Archaeological Society
- Dickins, Bruce, (Ed.), 1950, *The Place-Names of Cumberland*
- Donald, Thomas, 1770–1, *County of Cumberland Map*
- Greenwood, 1823, *Map of Cumberland*
- Heaton Cooper, W., 1960, *The Tarns of Lakeland*
- Nicolson, Joseph; Burn, Richard, 1777, *The History and Antiquities of the Counties of Cumberland and Westmorland*, Volume II
- Richardson, Autumn; Skelton, Richard, 2010, *Wolf Notes*
- Sedgefield, W.J., 1915, *The Place-Names of Cumberland and Westmorland*
- Speed, John, 1610, *Map of Cumberland*
- Various, 1769, *Manorial Title Deeds*
- Walcott, Mackenzie E. C., 1860, *A Guide to the Mountains, Lakes and North-West Coast of England*
- Warriner, Frank, 1926, *Some South Cumberland Place-Names*, Transactions of the Cumberland & Westmorland Antiquarian & Archaeological Society, NS XXVI
- Whaley, Diana, 2006, *A Dictionary of Lake District Place-Names*

OF THE ELM DECLINE

2 0 1 5

1.

LIST OF FIGURES

a wyrm came	a crawling
with the uses of fire to make	charcoal dust
the *tranchet* axe	and the book of pollen
from flint	stones
roots great and small	from forest clearances
may all plants now	dwindle to the root
I alone know	of a running stream

Assembled and adapted from *Aspects of Anglo-Saxon Magic*, by Bill Griffiths (1996),
Studies in the Vegetation History of the British Isles, edited by D. Walker & R.G. West (1970)

2.

a small island close to the southern shore

is formed of

[a]

bread and cheese

[b]

the smallest portion of milk or whey

[c]

the brink of famine

Assembled from *Tarns of the Central Lake District*,

by Haworth, de Boer, Evans, Osmaston, Pennington, Smith, Storey & Ware (2003),

The Village Labourer 1760–1832,

by J.L. Hammond & Barbara Hammond (1911)

3.

Stadial

parish machinery

signs of scouring

Artemisia

punctures the bark or skin

becoming winged creatures

Assembled from *Tarns of the Central Lake District*,
by Haworth, de Boer, Evans, Osmaston, Pennington, Smith, Storey & Ware (2003),
The Village Labourer 1760–1832, by J.L. Hammond & Barbara Hammond (1911),
The Trees of Old England, by Leo H. Grindon (1870)

4.

AGES B.C.	SURVEY	OF	THE	LAKES
	a	great		
			ditch	
				a tumulus
				a cist
		stones	so sunk	
	heart	of		
		mountains		
			in circles	
				and cairns

Assembled from *Lake District History*, *Chapter I*, *Ages B.C.*,

by W.G. Collingwood (1928)

5.

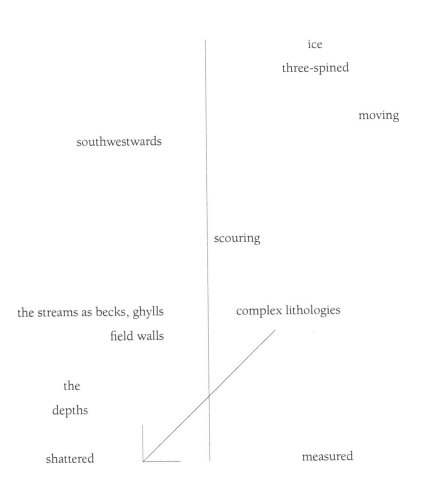

Assembled from *Tarns of the Central Lake District*,
by Haworth, de Boer, Evans, Osmaston, Pennington, Smith, Storey & Ware (2003)

6.

INTERSTADIAL

Calluna moor:

soil and litter

striving

deeper burrowing

the traps are sunk

concealed at depths

survivorship curves

Assembled from *Methods of Study in Quantitative Soil Ecology*,
edited by J. Phillipson (1971)

7.

i. Open and Common Fields

ii. Meadows and Pastures

iii. Commonable and Intermixed Lands

iv. A Tract of Waste Ground

The wolf's haugr, howe or hill

'I have no cage big enough for such a bird'

Adapted from *The Village Labourer* 1760–1832,
by J.L. Hammond & Barbara Hammond (1911)

8.

Ulmus

[a]

that which was lost

[b]

now found

[c]

resurgent

OF THE ELM DECLINE

by Richard Skelton, 2015

NOTE

Assembled and adapted from a variety of sources. See individual footnotes.

BIBLIOGRAPHY

°   Collingwood, W.G., 1928, *Lake District History*

°   Griffiths, Bill, 1996, *Aspects of Anglo-Saxon Magic*

°   Grindon, Leo H., 1870, *The Trees of Old England*

°   Hammond, J.L.; Hammond, Barbara, 1911, *The Village Labourer 1760–1832*

°   Haworth, de Boer, Evans, Osmaston, Pennington, Smith, Storey & Ware, 2003, *Tarns of the Central Lake District*

°   Phillipson, J., (Ed.), 1971, *Methods of Study in Quantitative Soil Ecology*

°   Walker, D.; West, R.G., (Eds.), 1970, *Studies in the Vegetation History of the British Isles*

THE MEDICINE EARTH

2 0 1 5

I.

'some places readily rotteth if one carelessly tendeth it'

surfeit earth (unrooted emptied)
wind-tongue pressing torn strata

hills hounded ripe with absence

cranes-bill yellow-skins red-wrack

characteristics:

wind ear campion cuckoo
felled stones triturated
unearthed cold

cavities hive quarried fauna
sky lifted emptied
harvesting their rages
bracken tramping the hedge raw [1]

II.

all fertile made waste
barren oak skin
salt anthers
bordered by minute teeth

and þæm laðan þe geond lond fereð
and the harmful one that throughout the land roams

makes here his cot
and a grave for wolves, foxes, harts [2]

warmed together in waste places the swarthened body [3]
covers vast tracts of land
now male or barren, much divided,
often white or grey

and the harmful one that throughout the land roams
moves his deadened limbs
with swine grease, sheep grease, [4]
butter and sulfur

NOTES & TOPOGRAPHICAL REFERENCES

Ordnance Survey grid references are in brackets. See *A Partial Gazetter* for etymological notes on place-names.

1. BRACKEN: BRACKENTHWAITE (SD1792).
2. WOLVES: ULGRA BECK (SD1895), ULPHA (SD1993), ULPHA BRIDGE (SD1993), ULPHA FELL (SD2098), WHELPSTY HOW (SD1791).
    FOXES: FOX BIELD (SD1898), FOXBIELD MOSS (SD1998), FOX CRAGS (SD1593).
    HARTS: BUCK CRAG (SD2299), HARTER FELL (SD2199), HARTLEY CRAG (SD1899).
3. SWARTHENED: Archaic. 'Of swarthened and deadened body. The disease cometh oftenest of corrupt humours after the inflammation of the disease which has passed away, the body whilom become swarthy.' [*Leechdoms, Wortcunning, and Starcraft of Early England*, Oswald Cockayne, 1865]
4. SWINE: SWINSTY HOW (SD2398).
    SHEEP: FAR HILL (SD1997).

with onlayings of barley [5]
incense of beorc, of bjarkan, burning, [6]
often trembling on their slender stalks
white bark of the trunk readily peeling

(from the deadened place a chant
from the swarthened body
a scarifying chant

this shall be whole
as far as the quick chanting of the lark
as far as the quick spittle of the rill
as far as the quick blowing of the wind
                                        over the wounded parts
this shall be whole again)

warmed together in waste places
so that there be nought remaining of the dead flesh
neither iron nor fire enduring [7]
soon to cut away all the dead and unfeeling flesh
out little spear, if it be here within

'I alone know of a running stream
where adders keep guard' [8]

5. BARLEY: BIGERT MIRE (SD1792), BIGERTMIRE PASTURE (SD1793).

6. BEORC, BJARKAN (I.E. *birch*): BIRKER FELL (SD1797 & SD2100), BIRKER FORCE (SD1899), BIRKERTHWAITE (SD1798), BIRKS (SD2399), LOW BIRKER POOL (SD1899), LOW BIRKER TARN (SD1899).

7. IRON: IRON CRAG (SD2197), IRON GROVES (SD1492).

8. ADDERS: GREAT WORM CRAG (SD1996) LITTLE WORM CRAG (SD1997), WORMSHELL HOW (SD2097).

river, when you drive the plough forth and cut the first furrow:
hold the water long in the mouth
wean and draw the blood from the deadened place
pound all to dust
mingle with honey
effect a cure with that

a terminal corymb
a yellow disc
creeping underground
in pastures, meadows, waste places

bogs and wet moors
glabrous and shining

ut lytel spere
leaves all green
creeping

the worm turneth to earth
the patient will be whole
again

III.

and the harmful one that throughout the land roams
moves his calyx tongue:

'bind the fox by its gloves, its glófa,[9]
holly-chain the kite, lapwing, dove and crane[10]
tie them to the land –
the raven, crow and blackcock[11]
made of Cumbric duß[12]
bind them too'

the grey absence of birch
the wind, untethered, jawbones –
acres drift
heather veins itself
springs wild skin:

recovery rills (centuries emptied)
ripple drafts
small mile of riverfat, lime-fed,[13]
blooding
the birch-grey absence
this shall be whole

barren stock
striated short organs
skin of dominion
this shall be whole

apparition wind
weather learned from washed soils
a bald stone bends, repopulates

flashed birth of rills
small, green inner lands
(the pteron has taken wing) [14]

9. BIND: Stone fox traps have been found in the Dunnerdale Fells above Ulpha Park (SD1891). See *Transactions of the Cumberland and Westmorland Antiquarian and Archaeological Society*, Volume XCVIII, 1998.

10. HOLLY: HOLLIN HOW (SD2297). 'Holly-chain' refers to the practice of using holly to make birdlime – an adhesive substance used to trap birds. 'In the north of England, holly was formerly so abundant in the Lake District that birdlime was made from it in large quantities.' [*A Modern Herbal*, M. Grieve, 1931].
    KITE: KITT HOW (SD1696).
    LAPWING: TEWIT MOSS (SD1697).
    DOVE: DOW CRAG (SD2099).
    CRANE: CORNEY FELL (SD1391).

11. RAVEN: RAINSBARROW WOOD (SD1993), RAVEN CRAG (SD1396 & SD1498).
    CROW: CROWBERRY HILL (SD2095), CROWHOW END (SD2200). *Crowberry*, a dwarf evergreen shrub with edible fruit, *Empetrum nigrum*.
    BLACKCOCK: COCKLEY MOSS (SD1695).

12. DUß: DEVOKE WATER (SD1596) cf. Cumbric **duß*, **dü*, 'black'.

13. LIME: LINBECK BRIDGE (SD1498), LINBECK GILL (SD1497).

14. PTERON: Bracken *Pteridium*, cf. Latin *pteris*, Greek *pteron* 'a wing'.

IV.

soil of echoes
soil of barely places
gore and flower
pike-like, clotting

a tall coarse weed of unknown origin
vigorous upright spreading
from the eye of the lake to the flesh of the hills
green inner barks
stripped from the young and suffered to ferment

consisting of pores and capillitium
fine thread-like fibres
discharged through the bursting of the skin
the smoke produced will stupefy
affording relief

five to eleven strong fibrous ribs
will stay the bleeding of minor wounds

bloodwort, woundwort, knitbone, scabious,
snapweed, touch-me-not
(taste astringent, odour none)

a wash for ulcers and wounds
tracts of broken land
a poultice to remove proud flesh

violet a tall coarse weed of unknown origin
violet vigorous upright spreading
violet from the eye of the lake to the flesh of hills

the worm turneth to earth
the patient will be whole
again

THE MEDICINE EARTH

by Autumn Richardson & Richard Skelton, 2015

NOTES

Includes material assembled from Bentham & Hooker, Cockayne, Grieve and Wren.

BIBLIOGRAPHY

° Bentham, George; Hooker, J.D., 1937, Handbook of the British Flora

° Cockayne, Oswald, 1865, *Leechdoms, Wortcunning, and Starcraft of Early England*

° Dickins, Bruce, (Ed.), 1950, *The Place-Names of Cumberland*

° Ekwall, Eilert, 1922, *The Place-Names of Lancashire*

° Fleming, Peter, 1998, *Stone Fox Traps, Borrans and Goose Bields*, Transactions of the Cumberland and Westmorland Antiquarian and Archaeological Society, Volume XCVIII

° Grieve, M., 1931, *A Modern Herbal*

° Whaley, Diana, 2006, *A Dictionary of Lake District Place-Names*

° Wren, R.C., 1923, *Potter's Cyclopaedia of Botanical Drugs and Preparations*

THWAITE

2017

HAZEL-THWAITE

A S E L

H Æ S E L   H Æ S E L

H Æ S L   H Æ S L

H A I S E L   H A I S E L

H A S A L A   H A S A L A

H A S A L Ô   H A S A L Ô

H A S E L   H A S E L

H Ā S E L   H Ā S E L

H A S E L L E   H A S E L L E

H A S E L O   H A S E L O

H A S L   H A S L

H A S L A   H A S L A

H A S L E   H A S L E

H A S S I L L E   H A S S I L L E

H A Z E L   H A Z E L

H A Z Z E L   H A Z Z E L

H E S E L   H E S E L

H E S E L L E   H E S E L L E

H E S L I   H E S L I

H E Z Z I L   H E Z Z I L

H E Z Z L E   H E Z Z L E

H I Z Z E L   H I Z Z E L

K O S E L O

ASH-THWAITE

```
            ÆSC
    ÆSCAS        ÆSCAS
      AICH          AICH
        AIS            AIS
          AISSE          AISSE
        AISSH          AISSH
      AISSHE           AISSHE
      ASCH             ASCH
        ASH              ASH
    ASKA               ASKA
  ASKIZ              ASKIZ
        ASKR       ASKR
        ASSE       ASSE
          ASSH             ASSH
            ASSHE          ASSHE
          EISCH          EISCH
        EISSE            EISSE
        ESH              ESH
            ESK            ESK
        ESSH             ESSH
          ESSHE             ESSHE
            EX             EX
          HAIS           HAIS
            HAS         HAS
          HESS       HESS
                        OS
```

WILLOW-THWAITE

VALIGA
VELIGÔ   VIÐ
VIÐIR   VIÐJA
VILOU   WALLER
WEL   WELEU
WELI   WELIG
WELIG   WELIGE
WELO   WELOGH
WELOU

WELOWE
WELU   WELUE
WELWE   WETHE
WHILUH   WIDDY
WIÐEN   WIÐI
WIÐIG   WILE   WILGE
WILGHE   WILH   WILIG
WILLE   WILLO   WILLOW
WILLOWE   WILLU   WILLUGH
WILO   WILOGH
WILOU   WILOUGH
WILOW   WILOWE
WILU   WILUG
WILUGH   WILWE
WITH

WITHE
WITHEN   WITHTH
WITHTHE   WITHY
WIÞÞE   WUDDY
WYTHINS

BIRCH-THWAITE

BEORC

BERC BERC

BERK-JŌN BERK-JŌN

BERKIÔ   BERKIÔ

BERKIÔN   BERKIÔN

BERKÔ   BERKÔ

BHERƎG

BIRCE

BIRCH

BIRCHE

BIRCHEN

BIRK

BIRK-TREE

BIRKE   BIRKE

BIRKI   BIRKI

BIRTH   BIRTH

BJÖRK   BJÖRK

BÖRK   BÖRK

BRECHE   BRECHE

BURK-TREE

BYRC

THWAITE

by Richard Skelton, 2017

NOTES

Thwaite, ON *þveit* 'clearing'.

Commissioned by Adrian Cooper for the *Little Toller* publication, *Arboreal*.

FURNESS FELLS

2 0 1 7

I.

between hills
where wolves played
between two furrows
at the point that
divides
high ground
and low ground
the road lying between
a line of feathers
a tenement now lost

Forget:

    ice patterns
    on the blind tarn

    giant's grave
    deep in the moss

    the wind's
    never ceasing tongue

    the deep hole
    in the river

Wake:

    the ancient river name

    the burnt tree stump

    the wyrm's cist

    the swallow's copse

yarrow
juniper
wormwood

mile upon mile
lift from the opened veins of hills

move with the sun's blood

birch
heather
rowan

mile upon mile
lift from the opened veins of hills

move with the sun's blood

rugged valley
may all your roots
become winged

II.

The following list of 48 toponyms from the upland area between Eskdale and Dunnerdale allude, in some way or other, to the flora or fauna of south-west Cumbria. The left hand column gives the current placename and its etymological roots, generally either in Old English or Old Norse. Where there is both an Old English and Old Norse word, the Old Norse has been preferred, as an acknowledgement of the profound effect of Scandinavian languages upon Cumbrian toponymy. It is important to note that the etymology does not imply an original spoken or written form for each toponym, as in some cases the etymology spans more than one language or time period. For example: *hjartar lēah cragge* (Harltey Crag) comprises Old Norse (*hjartar*), Old English (*lēah*) and Middle English (*cragge*). Fuller etymological information can be found in *A Partial Gazetteer*.

BIGERT MIRE
bygg mýrr

BIRKER FELL
birki ærgi fjall

BRACKENTHWAITE
brake þveit

BUCK CRAG
bukkr cragge

COCKLEY MOSS
cocc lēah mos

CORNEY FELL
cran ēg fjall

CROWBERRY HILL
crāwe beger hyll

CROWHOW END
crāwe haugr ende

DOG HOW
docga haugr

DOW CRAG
dúfa cragge

ELLERBECK BRIDGE
elri bekkr bryggja

FAR HILL
fár hallr

marsh by the barley fields

hill of the shieling by the birch trees

clearing where bracken grows

rocky height of the deer

marsh by the woodcock's clearing

hill of the heron's island

hill of crowberries

summit of the crow's hill

hill of the dog wolf

scar of the doves

bridge over the stream of alders

hill of the ewe

FOX BIELD
fox belde

GATE CRAG
gat cragge

GRASSGUARDS GILL
gras garðr gil

GREAT WHINSCALE
grēat whin skáli

GREAT WORM CRAG
grēat wyrm cragge

HARE GILL
hara gil

HARE RAISE
hara reisa

HARTER FELL
hjartar fjall

HARTLEY CRAG
hjartar lēah cragge

HAZEL HEAD
hæsel hēafod

HESK FELL
hesgen fjall

HESK FELL
eski fjall

fox's earth

scar of the goat

stream by the grassy enclosure

shieling of the gorse

great scar of the snake

stream of the hare

cairn-hill of the hare

mountain of the red deer

scar by the deer clearing

hill of hazels

hill of sedge

hill of ash

HESK FELL
hestr fjall

HOLLIN HOW
holegn haugr

HORSEHOW CRAGS
hross haugr cragge

KEPPLE CRAG
kapall cragge

KITT HOW
cyta haugr

LINBECK GILL
lind bekkr gil

LITTLE WORM CRAG
lytel wyrm cragge

MART CRAG
mearð cragge

OX PIKE
oxi pík

RAINSBARROW WOOD
hræfn berg wudu

RAVEN CRAG
hræfn cragge

ROWANTREE BECK
reynir trēo bekkr

hill of the horse

cairn-hill of the holly

cliffs by the horse's hill

scar of the horse

hill of the red kite

stream of the linden tree

small scar of the snake

scar of martens

hill summit of the ox

wood by the raven's hill

scar of ravens

stream by the mountain ash

STORTHES GILL
storð gil

SWINSTY HOW
svín haugr

TEWIT MOSS
tewet mosi

THORN HOW
þorn haugr

ULGRA BECK
ulfr grọf bekkr

ULPHA FELL
ulfr haugr fjall

WALLOWBARROW HEALD
wealwian berg held

WHIN RIGG
whin hryggr

WHINCOP
whin cop

WITHE BOTTOM
wīðig botm

WORMSHELL HOW
wyrm skáli haugr

YOADCASTLE
jalda castel

stream by the brushwood

hill of the pig sty

marsh of the lapwing

hill of hawthorns

stream by the wolf traps

hill of the wolf

hill of the deer wallow

ridge of gorse

summit of gorse

valley of willow

shieling on the hill of the snake

fort of the horse

A PARTIAL GAZETTEER

Ordnance Survey grid references in parentheses
Etymological details in square brackets
See bibliography for source texts

Br Brittonic	Mod. *Modern English*
Cm Cumbric	Mx *Manx*
Co *Cornish*	Nr *Norwegian*
Dial. *Cumbrian dialect*	OE *Old English*
Dn *Danish*	OFr *Old French*
Du *Dutch*	OIr *Old Irish*
Gl *Gaelic*	Sc *Scots*
Ir *Irish*	Sw *Swedish*
Lt *Lt*	W *Welsh*
ME *Middle English*	

ACRE GATE (SD1994) [OE *æcer* 'tilled field, open land' | OE *geat* 'gate'.]

ALMSHOUSES, THE (SD1993) [OE *ælmesse* 'alms' | OE *hūs* 'house'.]

ARMINGHOW GILL (SD1899) The meaning is obscure. [Mod? *arming* | ON *haugr* 'hill, mound, barrow' (Dial. *how, howe, haw*) | ON *gil* 'ravine, stream'.]

BARNSCAR (SD1395) Possibly, 'cairn of the woodland'. [Dial. *borran* 'cairn, pile of stones' | ON *skógr*, OE *sceaga* 'wood'. Also called BARNESKER, BARDSKEW & BARNSEA.]

BASIN BARROW (SD2297) 'Hill by the basin'. [Mod. *basin* | OE *berg* 'hill, tumuli'.]

BASKELL FARM (SD1993) 'Shieling of the cowshed', or 'Áskell's farm'. [ON *báss* 'cowshed' | ON *skáli* 'shieling', or ON *bú* 'farmstead, estate' | *Áskell* an ON personal name.]

BIGERT MIRE (SD1792) Possibly, 'marsh by the barley fields'. [ON *bygg* 'barley fields' | ON *mýrr* (Dial. *mire*) 'bog, marsh'.]

BIGERTMIRE PASTURE (SD1793) [BIGERT MIRE + OFr *pasture*.]

BIRKBY FELL (SD1496) 'Hill of the settlement of the Britons', from the old spelling BRETTEBY. [ON *breta, bretar* 'Britons, Welsh' | ON *bœr, bý* 'farmstead, settlement' | ON *fell* 'a single prominence' and *fjall* 'a mountainous region'.]

BIRKER FELL (SD1797 & SD2100) 'Hill of the shieling by the birch trees'. [ON *birki* 'birch trees' | Gaelic-Norse *ærgi, erg* 'shieling' | ON *fell* 'a single prominence' and *fjall* 'a mountainous region'.]

BIRKER FORCE (SD1899) [BIRKER + ON *fors* 'waterfall'.]

BIRKERTHWAITE (SD1798) [BIRKER + ON *þveit* 'clearing'.]

BIRKS (SD2399) [ON *birki* 'birch trees'.]

BLACK BECK (SD1496, SD1597, SD1698 & SD2300) 'Black stream' or 'pale stream'. [OE *blæc* 'black' or OE *blāc* 'pale' | ON *bekkr* 'stream'.]

BLACK CRAG (SD1897) 'Black scar' or 'pale scar'. [OE *blæc* 'black' or OE *blāc* 'pale' | ME *cragge* 'rock outcrop, cliff, scar' (cf. W *craig* 'rock, stone, boulder', *crogen* 'jaw', *crogi* 'to hang' | Mx *creg* | Sc & Ir *creag* | OIr *crec* 'rock' and *carrac* 'cliff'.)]

BLEAK HAW (SD1993) 'The bleak, exposed hill' or 'pale hill'. [ON *bleikr* 'pale' | ON *haugr* 'hill, mound, barrow' (Dial. *how, howe, haw*).]

BRACKENTHWAITE (SD1792) 'Clearing where bracken grows'. [Mod. *bracken* | Dial. *brake* (cf. Sw *bräken*, Dn *bregne*) | ON *þveit* 'clearing'.]

BRANDY CRAG (SD2298) [Du *brandewijn* ('burnt' or 'distilled wine') 'brandy' | ME *cragge* 'rock outcrop, cliff, scar'.]

BRANT RAKE (SD1498) 'The steep drove path'. [ON *brattr* 'steep' | ON *reika* (*reika* 'to wander', *reik* 'parting of the hair', *reið-gata* 'a riding-way, bridle-path', *vrēka* 'to drive'), OE *hraca, hrace* 'throat, pass'.]

BRANTRAKE CRAGS (SD1498) 'Cliffs by the steep drove path'. [BRANT RAKE + ME *cragge* 'rock outcrop, cliff, scar'.]

BRANTRAKE MOSS (SD1598) [BRANT RAKE + OE *mos*, ON *mosi* 'bog, marsh'.]

BRIGHOUSE (SD1994) 'The house by the bridge'. [OE *brycg*, ON *bryggja* 'bridge' | OE *hūs* 'house'.]

BROAD CRAG (SD1997) 'The broad rocky eminence'. [OE *brād*, ON *breiðr* 'broad' | ME *cragge* 'rock outcrop, cliff, scar'.]

BROWN RIGG (SD1896) 'The ridge of brown hills'. [OE *brūn*, ON *brúnn* | ON *hryggr* 'ridge'.]

BUCK CRAG (SD2299) 'Rocky height of the deer'. [OE *bucc*, ON *bukkr* 'roe deer or goat' | ME *cragge* 'rock outcrop, cliff, scar'.]

BURN MOOR (SD1492) 'Moor of the spring water', or 'the moor of cairns'. [OE *burna*, ON *brunnr* 'spring, stream' or OE *burgæsn*, ME *burghan(es)*, *borghan(es)* 'borran, burial, cairn' | OE *mōr*, ON *mór* 'moor'.]

BURNMOOR STAKE (SD1492) [BURN MOOR + OE *staca* 'stake'.]

CASTLE HOW (SD2300) [OE *castel* 'castle' | ON *haugr* 'hill, mound, barrow' (Dial. *how*, *howe*, *haw*).]

CASTLEHOW BECK (SD2300) [CASTLE HOW + ON *bekkr* 'stream'.]

CHURCH HOUSE (SD1993) [OE *cirice*, ON *kirkja* (Dial. *kirk*) 'church' | OE *hūs* 'house'.]

CLOSE, THE (SD2399) 'The enclosure'. [ME *close*, OFr *clos*, Lt *clausus* 'enclosure'.]

COCKLEY MOSS (SD1695) 'Marsh by the woodcock's clearing'. [OE *cocc* 'woodcock, blackcock' | OE *lēah* 'woodland clearing' | OE *mos*, ON *mosi* 'bog, marsh'.]

CORNEY FELL (SD1391) 'Hill of the heron's island'. [OE *cran*, *cron* 'heron, crane' | OE *ēg* 'island' | ON *fell* 'a single prominence' and *fjall* 'a mountainous region'.]

CROOK CRAGS (SD2399) [ON *krókr*, ME *crok(e)* 'hook, bend, corner of land' | ME *cragge* 'rock outcrop, cliff, scar'.]

CROOK WOOD (SD2095) [CROOK + OE *wudu*, ME *wode*.]

CROSBY GILL (SD1994) Possibly, 'stream near the settlement of the cross'. [ON *kross* 'cross' | ON *bær*, *bý* 'farmstead, settlement' | ON *gil* 'ravine, stream'.]

CROSBYTHWAITE (SD1994) [CROSBY + ON *þveit* 'clearing'.]

CROSBYTHWAITE BRIDGE (SD1895) [CROSBY + OE *brycg*, ON *bryggja* 'bridge'.]

CROWBERRY HILL (SD2095) 'Hill of crowberries'. [OE *crāwe* 'crow' | OE *beger* 'berry' (Crowberry, a dwarf evergreen shrub with edible fruit, *Empetrum nigrum*) | OE *hyll*, ON *hallr* 'hill'.]

CROWHOW END (SD2200) 'Summit of the crow's hill'. [OE *crāwe* 'crow' | ON *haugr* 'hill, mound, barrow' (Dial. *how*, *howe*, *haw*) | OE *ende* 'end'.]

DEMMING CRAG (SD2200) The meaning is obsure. [Mod. *demming* | ME
  cragge 'rock outcrop, cliff, scar'.]

DEVOKE WATER (SD1596) Possibly, 'the black water'. [Br **dubāco*, **dubācā* (cf.
  Cm**duß*, **dū* 'black') | OE *wæter* 'water'.]

DOD KNOTT (SD2100) 'The rounded hill'. [ME *dod(d)* 'rounded summit' | OE
  cnotta, ON *knottr*, *knút(r)* 'hill, height, crag'.]

DOG HOW (SD2196) Possibly, 'hill of the dog (-fox or -wolf)'. [OE *docga* 'dog-
  fox or wolf' | ON *haugr* 'hill, mound, barrow' (Dial. *how, howe, haw*).]

DOW CRAG (SD2099) 'Scar of the doves'. [OE *dūfe*, ON *dúfa* 'dove, pigeon' |
  ME *cragge* 'rock outcrop, cliff, scar'.]

DROPPING CRAG (SD2299) 'Promontory of the steep fall'. [Mod. *dropping* | ME
  cragge 'rock outcrop, cliff, scar'.]

DUDDON, RIVER (SD2093) Possibly, 'the black river', or a personal name
  Dudd(a). [Cm **duß*, **dū* 'black'.]

DUNNERDALE (SD1993) Possibly, 'valley of the Duddon', and therefore 'valley
  of the black river'. [Cm **duß*, **dū* 'black' | ON *dalr* 'valley'.]

DUNNERDALE FOREST (SD2298) [DUNNERDALE + OFr *forest*.]

ELLERBECK BRIDGE (SD1798) 'Bridge over the stream of alders'. [ON *elri(r)*
  'alder-copse' | OE *brycg*, ON *bryggja* 'bridge'.]

FAR HILL (SD1997) 'Hill of the ewe' or 'distant hill'. [OE *feorr*, ON *fjarre* 'far' or
  ON *fár, fé* 'sheep' | OE *hyll*, ON *hallr* 'hill'.]

FICKLE CRAG (SD2297) Possibly, 'the treacherous cliff'. [OE *ficol*, *befician* 'to
  deceive' | ME *cragge* 'rock outcrop, cliff, scar'.]

FOX BIELD (SD1898) 'Fox's earth'. [OE *fox* | ME *belde* 'dwelling' (cf. OE *beldo*
  'boldness, security', *boðl* 'dwelling').]

FOXBIELD MOSS (SD1998) 'Marsh by the fox's earth'. [FOX BIELD + OE *mos*, ON
  mosi 'bog, marsh'.]

FOX CRAGS (SD1593) 'Scar of the fox'. [FOX + ME *cragge* 'rock outcrop, cliff,
  scar'.]

FREEZE BECK (SD1896) 'The stream that freezes'. [OE *freosan*, ON *frjosa* 'to
  freeze' | ON *bekkr* 'stream'.]

GARNER BANK (SD1598) Possibly a personal name. [ON *banki* 'bank'.]

GATE CRAG (SD1899) 'Scar of the goat'. [OE *gat*, ON *geit* 'goat' | ME *cragge* 'rock outcrop, cliff, scar'.]

GRASSGUARDS (SD2298) 'The grassy enclosure'. [OE *gres*, *gras* | ON *garðr* 'yard, fence']

GRASSGUARDS GILL (SD2198) 'Stream by the grassy enclosure'. [GRASSGUARDS + ON *gil* 'ravine, stream'.]

GRAY STONE (SD1997) [OE *græg*, ON *grár* 'grey' | OE *stān*, ON *stein(n)* (Dial. *stayne*, *stain*) 'stone'.]

GREAT ARMING HOW (SD1899) The meaning is obscure. [OE *grēat* 'great' | Mod? *arming* | ON *haugr* 'hill, mound, barrow' (Dial. *how*, *howe*, *haw*).]

GREAT CRAG (SD1897) [GREAT + ME *cragge* 'rock outcrop, cliff, scar'.]

GREAT GILL (SD1795) [GREAT + ON *gil* 'ravine, stream'.]

GREAT WHINSCALE (SD1998) 'Shieling of the gorse'. [GREAT + ME *whin* (cf. ON **hvin*) 'whin, gorse' | ON *skáli* (Dial. *scale*) 'shieling; summer pasture with shepherd's hut, milking shed, peat store or similar'.]

GREAT WOOD (SD2399) [GREAT + OE *wudu*, ME *wode* 'wood'.]

GREAT WORM CRAG (SD1996) 'Great scar of the snake'. [GREAT + OE *wyrm* 'snake/reptile, slow-worm, asp, adder' | ME *cragge* 'rock outcrop, cliff, scar'.]

GREEN CRAG (SD2098) [OE *grēne*, ON *grœnn* 'green' | ME *cragge* 'rock outcrop, cliff, scar'.]

GREEN HOW (SD2095, SD1898 & SD1799) [GREEN + ON *haugr* 'hill, mound, barrow' (Dial. *how*, *howe*, *haw*).]

GRIMCRAG (SD1994), Possibly, 'the haunted rock'. [OE *grima* 'spectre, haunting spirit, goblin' | ME *cragge* 'rock outcrop, cliff, scar'.]

GRIMECRAG BRIDGE (SD1994) Possibly, 'bridge by the haunted rock'. [GRIM(E)CRAG + OE *brycg*, ON *bryggja* 'bridge'.]

HALL BECK (SD1696) 'Stream by the hall'. [OE *heall*, ON *höll* 'hall' | ON *bekkr* 'stream'.]

HARE GILL (SD1698) 'Stream of the hare'. [OE *hara* 'hare' | ON *gil* 'ravine, stream'.]

HARE RAISE (SD1492) 'Cairn-hill of the hare'. [OE *hara* 'hare' | ON *reisa*, *hreysi*

(Dial. *raise*, cf. Dn *rōs*) 'cairn, cairn-hill, pile of stones'.]

HARTER FELL (SD2199) 'Mountain of the red deer'. [OE *heorot*, ON *hjartar*, *hjortr* 'red deer, stag'.]

HARTLEY CRAG (SD1899) Possibly, 'scar by the deer clearing', or a familial name. [OE *heorot*, ON *hjartar*, *hjortr* 'red deer, stag' | OE *lēah* 'woodland clearing' | ME *cragge* 'rock outcrop, cliff, scar'.]

HAWS, THE (SD1994) 'The hill'. [ON *haugr* 'hill, mound, barrow' (Dial. *how*, *howe*, *haw*).]

HAZEL HEAD (SD1994) 'Hill of hazels'. [OE *hæsl*, *hæsel*, ON *hasl* 'hazel' | OE *hēafod* 'head'.]

HEIGHT, THE (SD1996) 'The high place'. [OE *hieþu*, *hēah* 'highest point, heavens'.]

HESK FELL (SD1794) 'Hill of sedge', 'hill of ash', or 'hill of the horse'. [W *hesgen*, Co *heschen* 'sedge or coarse grass', or ON *askr*, *eski* 'ash tree' or ON *hestr* 'horse' | ON *fell* 'a single prominence' and *fjall* 'a mountainous region'.]

HIGH GROUND (SD1798) 'The high farm or land'. [OE *hieþu*, *hēah* 'highest point, heavens' | ON *grund* 'fertile land, valley bottom, farm'.]

HIGH STONYTHWAITE (SD2196) 'The high rocky clearing'. [HIGH + OE *stān*, ON *stein(n)* 'stone' | ON *þveit* 'clearing'.]

HIGHFORD BECK (SD1897) 'Stream of the high crossing'. [HIGH + OE *ford* 'river crossing' | ON *bekkr* 'stream'.]

HINNING HOUSE CLOSE (SD2399) 'The enclosure of the house'. [OE *hegning*, ME *haining* 'enclosed land' | OE *hūs* 'house' | ME *close*, OFr *clos*, Lt *clausus* 'enclosure'.]

HOLE HOUSE (SD1893) 'House in the hollow'. [OE *hol(h)*, ON *hol(r)* 'hollow' | OE *hūs* 'house'.]

HOLEHOUSE BRIDGE (SD1793) [HOLE HOUSE + OE *brycg*, ON *bryggja* 'bridge'.]

HOLEHOUSE GILL (SD1893) [HOLE HOUSE + ON gil 'ravine, stream'.]

HOLEHOUSE TARN (SD1593) [HOLE HOUSE + ON *tjorn*, ME *terne* 'small, mountain pool'.

HOLLIN HOW (SD2297) 'Cairn-hill of the holly'. [OE *holegn* 'holly' | ON *haugr* 'hill, mound, barrow' (Dial. *how, howe, haw*).]

HORSEHOW CRAGS (SD2200) 'Cliffs by the horse's hill'. [OE *hors*, ON *hross* 'horse' | ON *haugr* 'hill, mound, barrow' (Dial. *how, howe, haw*) | ME *cragge* 'rock outcrop, cliff, scar'.]

HOWS, THE (SD2399) 'The hills'. [ON *haugr* 'hill, mound, barrow' (Dial. *how, howe, haw*).]

IRON CRAG (SD2197) [OE *isærn*, ON *isarn* 'iron' | ME *cragge* 'rock outcrop, cliff, scar'.]

IRON GROVES (SD1492) Possibly, 'the iron pits'. [IRON + ON *gróf* 'pit' or OE *gráf* 'copse'.]

KEPPLE CRAG (SD1999) 'Scar of the horse'. [ON *kapall* 'horse' | ME *cragge* 'rock outcrop, cliff, scar'.]

KEPPLE CRAGS (SD2198) 'Cliffs of the horse'. [KEPPLE + CRAG.]

KITT HOW (SD1696) 'Hill of the red kite'. [OE *cyta* 'red kite' | ON *haugr* 'hill, mound, barrow' (Dial. *how, howe, haw*).]

KNOTT, THE (SD1495 & SD2196) 'The hill'. [OE *cnotta*, ON *knottr, knút(r)* 'hill, height, crag'.]

LAD HOW (SD2196) 'The cairn-hill'. [OE *hlæð*, ON *hlaði* 'pile or stack of stones' | ON *haugr* 'hill, mound, barrow' (Dial. *how, howe, haw*).]

LINBECK BRIDGE (SD1498) 'Bridge over the stream of the linden tree'. [OE *lind* 'linden tree' | ON *bekkr* 'stream' | OE *brycg*, ON *bryggja* 'bridge'.]

LINBECK GILL (SD1497) Possibly, 'ravine through which the stream of the flax tree flows', otherwise a tautology for 'stream of the linden tree'. [LINBECK + ON *gil* 'ravine, stream'.]

LITTLE ARMING HOW (SD1899) The meaning is obscure. [OE *lytel* 'little' | Mod? *arming* | ON *haugr* 'hill, mound, barrow' (Dial. *how, howe, haw*).]

LITTLE BECK (SD1797) [LITTLE + ON *bekkr* 'stream'.]

LITTLE CRAG (SD1897) [LITTLE + ME *cragge* 'rock outcrop, cliff, scar'.]

LITTLE GILL (SD1695) [LITTLE + ON *gil* 'ravine, stream']

LITTLE WORM CRAG (SD1997) 'Small scar of the snake'. [LITTLE + OE *wyrm* 'snake/reptile, slow-worm, asp, adder' | ME *cragge* 'rock outcrop, cliff, scar'.]

LONG CRAG (SD2098, SD2398 & SD2399) [OE *lang*, ON *langr* 'long' | ME *cragge* 'rock outcrop, cliff, scar'.]

LONG HILL (SD1997) [LONG + OE *hyll*, ON *hallr* 'hill'.]

LOW BIRKER POOL (SD1899) 'Slow stream near the shieling by the birch trees'.
[ON *lagr* 'low' | ON *birki* 'birch trees' | Gaelic-Norse *ærgi, erg* 'shieling' |
OE *pōl, pull*, W *pwll* 'pool' (cf. Dial. *low pool* 'slow stream'.)]

LOW BIRKER TARN (SD1999) [LOW BIRKER + ON *tjorn*, ME *terne* 'small,
mountain pool'.]

LOW GROUND (SD1798) [LOW + ON *grund* 'fertile land, valley bottom, farm'.]

LOW STONYTHWAI(TE) (SD2196) 'Clearing in the low, stony ground'. [LOW +
OE *stān*, ON *stein(n)* 'stone' | ON *þveit* 'clearing'.]

MAIDEN CASTLE (SD2299) The meaning is obscure. [Mod. *maiden* | OE *castel*
'castle'.]

MART CRAG (SD2299) 'Scar of martens'. [OE *mearð* 'marten' | ME *cragge* 'rock
outcrop, cliff, scar'.]

MEETING HILL (SD1997) [Mod. *meeting* | OE *hyll*, ON *hallr* 'hill'.]

MOOR HOUSE (SD2095) [OE *mōr*, ON *mór* 'moor' | OE *hūs* 'house'.]

OX PIKE (SD2197) 'Hill summit of the ox'. [OE *oxa*, ON *oxi* 'ox' | OE *pīc*, ON
pík 'pike, hill summit'.]

PEN, THE (SD2197) 'The hill'. [Cm **pen(n)* 'head, top, end' (cf. Gl *beann*
'mountain').]

PIKE, THE (SD1893 & SD1998) [OE *pīc*, ON *pík* 'pike, hill summit'.]

PIKE HOW (SD1697 & SD2399) 'The hill summit'. [PIKE + ON *haugr* 'hill,
mound, barrow' (Dial. *how, howe, haw*).]

PIKE HOW CLOSE (SD2399) [PIKE HOW + ME *close*, OFr *clos*, Lt *clausus*
'enclosure'.]

PIKE SIDE (SD1893) [PIKE + OE *side*.]

RAINSBARROW WOOD (SD1993) 'Wood by the raven's hill'. [OE *hræfn*, ON
hrafn 'raven' | OE *berg* 'hill, tumuli' | OE *wudu*, ME *wode* 'wood'.]

RAVEN CRAG (SD1396 & SD1498) 'Scar of ravens'. [OE *hræfn*, ON *hrafn* 'raven'
| ME *cragge* 'rock outcrop, cliff, scar'.]

RED GILL (SD1493 & SD1698) [OE *read*, ON *rauðr* 'red' | ON *gil* 'ravine,
stream'.]

REDGILL HEAD (SD1492) [RED + ON *gil* 'ravine, stream' | OE *hēafod* 'head'.]

RED SCAR (SD1896) [RED + ON *sker* (Dial. *scar, scaur*) 'escarpment, crag'.]

RIGG BECK (SD1596) 'The stream from the ridge'. [ON *hryggr* 'ridge' | ON *bekkr* 'stream'.]

ROUGH CRAG (SD1896 & SD1697) [OE *rūh* 'rough' | ME *cragge* 'rock outcrop, cliff, scar'.]

ROUGH HOW (SD1796) [ROUGH + ON *haugr* 'hill, mound, barrow' (Dial. *how, howe, haw*).]

ROWANTREE BECK (SD1997) 'Stream by the rowan tree (mountain ash)'. [ON *reynir* 'rowan' (cf. Sw *ronn*, Nr *raun,* Dial. *roan*) | OE *trēo(w)* 'tree' | ON *bekkr* 'stream'.]

ROWANTREE FORCE (SD1493) [ROWANTREE + ON *fors* 'waterfall'.]

ROWANTREE GILL (SD1493) [ROWANTREE + ON *gil* 'ravine, stream'.]

ROWANTREE HOW (SD1595 & SD2297) [ROWANTREE + ON *haugr* 'hill, mound, barrow' (Dial. *how, howe, haw*).]

SADDLEBACKED HOW (SD2300) 'The saddle-shaped hill'. [OE *sadol* 'saddle' | ON *haugr* 'hill, mound, barrow' (Dial. *how, howe, haw*).]

SCAR CRAG (SD1897) 'Cliff of the escarpments', something of a tautology. [ON *sker* (Dial. *scar, scaur*) 'escarpment, crag' | ME *cragge* 'rock outcrop, cliff, scar'.]

SEAT, THE (SD1697) 'Seat-like prominence' or 'the shieling'. [OE *sǣte*, ON *sǣti* 'high place or seat-like prominence' or ON *sǣtr* 'shieling'.]

SEAT HOW (SD1697) 'Hill of the seat-like prominence' or 'hill of the shieling'. [SEAT + ON *haugr* 'hill, mound, barrow' (Dial. *how, howe, haw*).]

SERGEANT CRAG (SD1493) Possibly, 'crag of the land-sergeant'. [Mod. *Sergeant* | ME *cragge* 'rock outcrop, cliff, scar'.]

SIKE MOSS (SD1896) 'Marsh of the small stream'. [OE *sīc*, ON *sík(i)* (Dial. *sike, syke*) 'narrow stream or gutter' | OE *mos*, ON *mosi* 'bog, marsh'.]

SILVER HOW (SD1998) 'Hill of silver'. [OE *seolfor*, ON *silfr* 'silver' | ON *haugr* 'hill, mound, barrow' (Dial. *how, howe, haw*).]

SKELLY CRAGS (SD2300) 'Cliffs by the shieling'. [ON *skáli* 'shieling' | ME *cragge* 'rock outcrop, cliff, scar'.]

SMALLSTONE BECK (SD1898) 'Stream of the small stones'. [OE *smæl* 'small' | OE *stān*, ON *stein(n)* 'stone' | ON *bekkr* 'stream'.]

SMITHY MIRE (SD1699) 'Marsh by the iron bloomery'. [OE *smiððe* 'iron bloomery, smithy' | ON *mýrr* (Dial. *mire*) 'bog, marsh'.]

SPOTHOW GILL (SD2099) Possibly, 'stream of the small hill'. [ON *spotti* 'small piece' | ON *haugr* 'hill, mound, barrow' (Dial. *how, howe, haw*) | ON *gil* 'ravine, stream'.]

STAINTON BECK (SD1494) 'Stream by the stone settlement'. [OE *stān*, ON *stein(n)* (Dial. *stayne, stain*) 'stone' | OE *tūn* 'settlement, farmstead' | ON *bekkr* 'stream'.]

STAINTON FELL (SD1494) 'Mountain by the stone settlement'. [STAINTON + ON *fell* 'a single prominence' and *fjall* 'a mountainous region'.]

STAINTON PIKE (SD1594) 'Hill summit by the stone settlement'. [STAINTON + OE *pīc*, ON *pík* 'pike, hill summit'.]

STANLEY FORCE (SD1799) Possibly a familial name, *Stanley*. [ON *fors* 'waterfall'.]

STORD'S HILL (SD1596) 'Summit of the brushwood'. [ON *storð* 'plantation, brushwood' | OE *hyll*, ON *hallr* 'hill'.]

STORTHES (SD1693) 'Brushwood'. [ON *storð* 'plantation, brushwood'.]

STORTHES GILL (SD1694) 'Stream by the brushwood'. [STORTHES + ON *gil* 'ravine, stream'.]

SWINSTY HOW (SD2398) 'Hill of the pig sty'. [OE *swīn*, ON *svín* 'pig, swine' | OE *sti* 'hall, pen' or ON *stia* 'sty, kennel' | ON *haugr* 'hill, mound, barrow' (Dial. *how, howe, haw*).]

TARN CRAG (SD1999) 'Scar of the small lake'. [ON *tjorn*, ME *terne* 'small, mountain pool' | ME *cragge* 'rock outcrop, cliff, scar'.]

TEWIT MOSS (SD1697) 'Marsh of the lapwing'. [OE *tewit, tewet* 'peewit, lapwing' | OE *mos*, ON *mosi* 'bog, marsh'.]

THORN HOW (SD1997) 'Hill of hawthorns'. [OE, ON *þorn* 'hawthorn' | ON *haugr* 'hill, mound, barrow' (Dial. *how, howe, haw*).]

TONGUE BECK (SD1792) 'Stream of the narrows'. [ON *tunga* 'narrow land' | ON *bekkr* 'stream'.]

TONGUESDALE MOSS (SD1699) 'Marsh of the narrow valley'. [TONGUE + ON *dalr* 'valley' | OE *mos*, ON *mosi* 'bog, marsh'.]

ULGRA BECK (SD1895) Possibly, 'Stream by the wolf traps'. [ON *ulfr* 'wolf' | ON *grǫf* 'pit' | ON *bekkr* 'stream'.]

ULPHA (SD1993) Either 'hill of the wolf' or 'Ulf's hill or barrow'. [ON *ulfr* 'wolf', or the personal name 'Ulf' | ON *haugr* 'hill, mound, barrow' (Dial. *how, howe, haw*).]

ULPHA BRIDGE (SD1993) [ULPHA + OE *brycg*, ON *bryggja* 'bridge'.]

ULPHA FELL (SD2098) Possibly, 'the high ground around the wolf's hill', otherwise a tautology. [ULPHA + ON *fell* 'a single prominence' and *fjall* 'a mountainous region'.]

UNDERBANK (SD1799) 'The place under the bank'. [OE *under* | ON *banki* 'bank'.]

WALLHEAD CRAG (SD2199) 'Scar of the wall's head'. [OE *wall* | OE *hēafod* 'head' | ME *cragge* 'rock outcrop, cliff, scar'.]

WALLOWBARROW COPPICE (SD2196) Possibly, 'trees by the hill of the deer wallow'. [OE *walla* 'pale' or OE *walu* 'ridge, embankment' or OE *wealwian* 'wallows' (baths of mud used by red deer) | OE *berg* 'hill, tumuli' | OFr *copeiz* 'coppice'.]

WALLOWBARROW HEALD (SD2197) Possibly, 'hill slope of the hill of the deer wallow', but likely a tautology. [WALLOWBARROW + OE *held* 'hill-slope'.]

WASHFOLD POINT (SD1697) [OE *wæsc* 'wash' | OE *fal(o)d* 'fold' | OFr *point*.]

WATER CRAG (SD1597) Possibly, 'escarpment by (Devoke) water'. [OE *wæter* 'water' | ME *cragge* 'rock outcrop, cliff, scar'.]

WATNESS COY (SD1596) Possibly, 'the cove by the promontory on the water'. [ON *vatn* 'water' | ON *nes* 'headland' or OE *næs* 'promontory' | OE *cofa* 'chamber, cell, cave' or OE *cop* 'cove, cave, chamber' or ON *kofi* 'hut, shed' – the sense meaning 'cove' is apparently later.]

WET GILL (SD2298) [OE *wæt* 'wet' | ON *gil* 'ravine, stream'.]

WHELPSTY HOW (SD1791) 'Cairn-hill of the wolf litter'. [OE *hvelpr* 'young dog or wolf' | OE *sti* 'hall, pen' or ON *stia* 'sty, kennel' | ON *haugr* 'hill, mound, barrow' (Dial. *how, howe, haw*).]

WHIN RIGG (sd1798) 'Ridge of gorse'. [ME *whin* (cf. ON **hvin*) 'whin, gorse' | ON *hryggr* 'ridge'.]

WHINCOP (sd1799) 'Summit of gorse'. [WHIN + OE *cop(p)* 'top' (cf. Gl *ceap* 'head, hill').]

WHINCOP BRIDGE (sd1798) [WHIN + OE *brycg*, ON *bryggja* 'bridge'.]

WHIS GILL (sd1699) The meaning is obscure. [Mod? *whis* | ON *gil* 'ravine, stream'.]

WHITE CRAG (sd1997) [OE *hwīt*, ON *hvítr* 'pale' | ME *cragge* 'rock outcrop, cliff, scar'.]

WHITE HOW (sd2097) [WHITE + ON *haugr* 'hill, mound, barrow' (Dial. *how, howe, haw*).]

WHITE MOSS (sd2097) [WHITE + OE *mos*, ON *mosi* 'bog, marsh'.]

WHITE PIKE (sd1595) [WHITE + OE *pīc*, ON *pík* 'pike, hill summit'.]

WHITE WALL (sd1896) [WHITE + OE *wall*.]

WHITFELL (sd1593) [WHIT(E) + ON *fell* 'a single prominence' and *fjall* 'a mountainous region'.]

WINDS GATE (sd1895) [OE *wind* | ON *gata* 'road, way, track'.]

WITHE BOTTOM (sd1593) 'Valley of willow'. [OE *botm*, ON *botn* 'valley' | OE *wīðig* 'willow'.]

WONDER HILL (sd1798) [Mod. *wonder* | OE *hyll*, ON *hallr* 'hill'.]

WOOD KNOTTS (sd1795) 'The wooded prominence'. [OE *wudu*, ME *wode* 'wood' | OE *cnotta*, ON *knottr*, *knút(r)* 'hill, height, crag'.]

WOODEND (sd1696) 'The end of the wood', or, 'the end of the township of the wood'. [WOOD + OE *ende* 'end'.]

WOODEND BRIDGE (sd1796) [WOODEND + OE *brycg*, ON *bryggja* 'bridge'.]

WOODEND HEIGHT (sd1595) [WOODEND + OE *hieþu*, *hēah* 'height'.]

WOODEND POOL (sd1796) [WOODEND + OE *pōl*, *pull*, W *pwll* 'pool']

WORMSHELL HOW (sd2097) Possibly, 'shieling on the hill of the snake'. [OE *wyrm* 'snake/reptile, slow-worm, asp, adder' | ON *skáli*, ME *schele* 'shieling' | ON *haugr* 'hill, mound, barrow' (Dial. *how, howe, haw*).]

YOADCASTLE (sd1595) 'Fort of the horse'. [Dial. *yoad, yad, yaad*, ON *jalda* 'horse' | OE *castel* 'castle'.]

FURNESS FELLS

by Autumn Richardson & Richard Skelton, 2017

NOTES

Commissioned by Colin Riley for *In Place*, an extended multi-media song-cylce exploring a 'sense of place' in the British Isles. *Part I* was subsequently adapted into a libretto. It has been included here in its original form. *A Partial Gazetteer* was originally compiled for *Wolf Notes*, Folio Edition, 2010.

BIBLIOGRAPHY

° Dickins, Bruce, (Ed.), 1950, *The Place-Names of Cumberland*

° Ekwall, Eilert, 1922, *The Place-Names of Lancashire*

° Heaton Cooper, W., 1960, *The Tarns of Lakeland*

° Nicolson, Joseph; Burn, Richard, 1777, *The History and Antiquities of the Counties of Cumberland and Westmorland*, Volume II

° Sedgefield, W.J., 1915, *The Place-Names of Cumberland and Westmorland*

° Walcott, Mackenzie E. C., 1860, *A Guide to the Mountains, Lakes and North-West Coast of England*

° Warriner, Frank, 1926, *Some South Cumberland Place-Names*, Transactions of the Cumberland & Westmorland Antiquarian & Archaeological Society, NS XXVI

° Whaley, Diana, 2006, *A Dictionary of Lake District Place-Names*

DISCOGRAPHY

Five albums of music, written and performed under the pseudonym *AR,
were created to accompany the texts contained in this volume.

- *Wolf Notes,* 2010
- *Succession,* 2013
- *Echoless,* 2013
- *Diagrams for the Summoning of Wolves,* 2015
- *Memorious Earth,* 2015

Lightning Source UK Ltd.
Milton Keynes UK
UKHW010945111220
374897UK00003B/503